The Poetry of Enlightenment

Books by Chan Master Sheng Yen

Attaining the Way: A Guide to the Practice
of Chan Buddhism

Complete Enlightenment: Zen Comments
on the *Sutra of Complete Enlightenment*

Dharma Drum: The Life and Heart
of Chan Practice

Faith in Mind: A Commentary
on Seng Ts'an's Classic

The Infinite Mirror: Commentaries
on Two Chan Classics

The Method of No-Method: The Chan
Practice of Silent Illumination

The Poetry of Enlightenment: Poems by
Ancient Chan Masters

Song of Mind: Wisdom from
the Zen Classic *Xin Ming*

The Poetry of Enlightenment

Poems by
Ancient Chan Masters

Chan Master Sheng Yen

Shambhala
Boston & London
2006

Calligraphy on opposite page by Master Sheng-yen:

"Through the tangles of vines and tendrils,
and the knots of cords and ropes . . . . .
the thread is not clear."

葛藤絡索

聖嚴

Shambhala Publications, Inc.
Horticultural Hall
300 Massachusetts Avenue
Boston, Massachusetts 02115
www.shambhala.com

Associate Editor: Karen Zinn; Assistant Editors: Earnest Heau, Alan
Rubinstein; Translators: Richard Halsted, Paul Kennedy, Peigwang Li,
Wei K. Shiue, Paul Truong, Karen Zinn; Transcribers: Nancy Patchen,
Karen Zinn; Calligraphy: Chan Master Sheng Yen, Nora Ling-yun Shih

Printed in United States of America

❀ This edition is printed on acid-free paper that meets the American
National Standards Institute Z39.48 Standard.
♻ Shambhala Publications makes every effort to print on recycled
paper. For more information visit www.shambhala.com.
Distributed in the United States by Random House, Inc., and in
Canada by Random House of Canada Ltd

Library of Congress Cataloging-in-Publication Data
The poetry of enlightenment: poems by ancient Chan Masters / [edited
by] Chan Master Sheng Yen.
   p.   cm.
Originally published: New York, N.Y.: Dharma Drum Publications,
©1987.
ISBN 978-1-59030-399-3 (alk. paper)
1. Zen poetry, Chinese—Translations into English. I. Shengyan, 1930–
II. Title: Poems by ancient Chan Masters.
BQ9264.4.C62P64 2006
294.3'4432—dc22
                                      2006045044

CONTENTS

Introduction

Some years ago I edited a book in Chinese entitled
Ch'an Men Hsiu Cheng Chih Yao, or *A Guide to the
Experience and Practice of Ch'an,* a collection of essays
and poems by Ch'an masters. The authors ranged
from Bodhidharma, the Indian monk who arrived in
China in 520 or 527 A.D., to Master Hsu Yun (1840-
1959). Of the twenty-four works in the collection,
thirteen are poems. I have selected eight of these for
the present volume plus two other poems, one by Han
Shan Te Ch'ing *(On Clear Mind),* and one by Hung
Chih Cheng Chueh *(Silent Illumination).* Three of our
ten poems can be found in the Wan Tzu Hsu Tsang
Ching *(Manji-zokuzokyo): Song of the Precious Mirror
Samadhi, On Clear Mind* and *Contemplating Mind. Silent
Illumination* is found in the *Ta Cheng Ta Tsang Ching
(Taisho-daizokyo).* The rest are recorded in the *Ching Te
Ch'uan Teng Lu (Record of the Transmission of the Lamp).*

I have used these same ten poems over the years
as lecture topics for Ch'an retreats and evening classes
at the Ch'an Meditation Center in New York City.
Before each lecture series one or more of my bilingual
students would render each poem into English as I

interpreted the meaning, line by line, in modern Chinese. The poems were chosen for their concise and simple language, but also for their deep and rich meanings. They were written by highly accomplished Ch'an masters only after they had reached thorough enlightenment. These masters wrote poems to express their experiences of Ch'an, to provide future generations with the means of realizing Ch'an, and to describe the situation of the mind after enlightenment.

But since Ch'an is basically ineffable, the authors relied heavily on allusions, similes and metaphors which can be interpreted in less obscure language only by someone who has already practiced Ch'an very deeply. I believe that in the English translation, the poems become more accessible; but even so, only a portion of the meanings may be easy to understand. The density of the ideas in the poems ideally requires an expanded commentary. Two of the poems — Han Shan's *Contemplating Mind* and Hung Chih's *Silent Illumination* — have already been published along with commentaries in my book *Getting the Buddha Mind*. Future books containing full commentaries on most of the other poems are planned.

My purpose in publishing this collection is to provide the reader with insight into the minds of the Ch'an masters — their practices and their post-enlightenment experiences. Moreover, the poets were not only highly accomplished practitioners, they were also well-versed in literature, history and Buddhist scholarship. In these poems we can discern references

2

to Chinese philosophical, religious and literary history, as well as to the roots and theories of Indian Buddhism.

In Chinese the poems vary in style. Some strictly follow the rules of Chinese poetry and others are written in the form of a song. Still others resemble the *gathas* (poems) of Sanskrit verse, although in Chinese the standard meter and rhyme of Sanskrit are not retained. Thus these poems are also interesting from the point of view of literary analysis, though it is not my purpose to elaborate on that aspect here.

To my knowledge there are no anthologies of Ch'an poetry in Chinese, Japanese or English which describe in detail the methods of practice and the experiences of Ch'an masters. Furthermore, there are few prose sources in English dealing with the same topics. On the other hand, there are numerous books in English that relate the episodes of the *kung-ans* (koans). The prevailing view that comes from reading these stories is that the practice of Ch'an is methodless, and since there is no way to describe the experience of Ch'an, it is suggested that we just go ahead and practice by studying the *kung-ans*. The purpose of these poems is different in that they specifically show you how to practice, what attitudes to cultivate and what pitfalls to beware of. Finally, they attempt to describe the ineffable experience of Ch'an itself. These poems flow directly from the minds of the enlightened Ch'an masters; we get a glimpse into their experience at the time of, and after their enlightenement. In contrast, in reading a *kung-an* we get an objective story of what happened and we don't really know what was in the minds of the participants.

It is my hope that this collection of poems will give those who are interested in the practice a new way of looking at Ch'an and a more balanced view of the scope of Ch'an literature. The present selection is offered to make this tradition available to Western readers, who may otherwise not be aware of its existence.

Master Sheng-yen
Ch'an Meditation Center
New York City
November, 1985

Calming the Mind

息 Hsi

心 Hsin

釋
亡
名

銘 Ming

Calming the Mind

by Shih Wang Ming (6c. A.D.)

We are not certain whether Wang Ming was the author's real name or just a pseudonym. In fact the term "wang ming" is often used to mean "anonymous." We do know that his lay surname was Sung and that he lived at the end of the Liang dynasty (502-556). Sung was known for his intelligence and talent. He served as a government official, but after the Liang dynasty ended he became a monk. Since he left home (took vows) with a Ch'an master, his practice followed that of the Ch'an sect. Perhaps because of his intellectual and scholarly background, he also studied Buddhist theory with numerous Dharma teachers.

Wang Ming's thought, reflected in his poem *Calming the Mind*, is quite different from the spirit of the Sixth Patriarch, Hui Neng, who represents the mainstream of Ch'an in China. In fact, the poem reveals that his thought was heavily influenced by the Taoist philosophers Lao Tzu and Chuang Tzu. For example, the exhortation not to listen to sounds or look at forms was taught by Lao Tzu. He also exhibits his leaning toward Taoist philosophy, or the naturalist approach, in the lines:

> *Through excessive thinking the will is weakened.*
> *The more one knows, the more the mind is confused.*

In the practice, he emphasizes unifying the mind (literally, holding to one). This is not typical of the thought of the subsequent development of Ch'an but goes back to the Indian *Sutra of the Buddha's Last Bequest (I Chiao Ching)* which speaks of putting the mind on one point *(chih hsin i ch'u)*.

Calming the Mind is an excellent poem to help the beginning practitioner. First, it shows us the basic method of practice. Second, it tells us how to practice this method. Third, it advises us to take a natural approach in our daily life, letting go of all worries and vexations.

Calming the Mind

Too much knowledge leads to overactivity;
Better to calm the mind.
The more you consider, the greater the loss;
Better to unify the mind.

Excessive thinking weakens the will.
The more you know, the more your mind is confused.
A confused mind gives rise to vexation.
The weakened will obstructs the Tao.

Don't say there is no harm in this;
The ensuing pain may last forever.
Don't think there is nothing to fear;
The calamities churn like bubbles in a boiling pot.

Water dripping ceaselessly
Will fill the four seas.
Specks of dust not wiped away
Will become the five mountains.[1]

Protect the branches to save the roots;
Though a small matter, it is not trivial.
Close the seven orifices,[2]
Shut off the six senses.[3]

Pay no heed to forms;
Do not listen to sounds.

Listening to sounds you become deaf,
Observing forms you become blind.

Literature and art
Are but busy gnats in the air;
Technique and ability
A solitary lamp in the sun.

Those able and talented ones
Are really stupid fellows.
Discarding the pure and simple
They drown in too much beauty.

Consciousness is an untamed horse,
The mind an unruly monkey.
If the spirit is overactive,
The body will sicken and die.

Wrong conduct ends in delusion;
Those treading this path become mired in mud.
To regard ability as precious
Is called confusion.

To exaggerate clumsiness and covet skill
Does not lead to great virtue.
Of much fame but little contribution,
Their reputations quickly crumble.

Merely reading books
Is of no lasting value.

CALMING THE MIND

Being inwardly proud
Brings the enmity of others.

Using speech
Or written words
To gain the praise of others
Is something most repulsive.

What common people regard as auspicious
The sage takes as evil.
The enjoyment gained is fleeting,
But the sorrow is everlasting.

Beware of shadows and tracks;
The farther you leave them, the better.
Sitting upright in the shade of a tree,
Neither traces nor shadows remain.

Worries of birth and distress of old age
Are products of your own thoughts.
If the mind's thinking is ended,
Birth and death are forever cut off.

Not dying, not born,
Without form or name,
The Tao is empty and tranquil.
The myriad phenomena are equal.

What is of value? What is cheap?
Where is there shame or glory?

THE POETRY OF ENLIGHTENMENT

What is excellent or inferior?
How can there be heavy and light?

The clear sky puts purity to shame.
No brightness compares with the brilliant sun.
Stable as Mount T'ai;
Steady as a golden wall.

I respectfully present this poem to all virtuous ones
So that this Tao will forever remain.

1. The five mountains in China having a sacred
   connection with Buddhism (analogous to the five
   sacred mountains of India): Ching Shan, Pei Shan,
   Nan Shan, King Asoka Shan, T'ai Po Shan.

2. The seven orifices: two eyes, two ears, two nostrils,
   and mouth.

3. The six senses: sight, hearing, smell, taste, touch
   and mental perception.

The Mind King

心 *Hsin*

王 *Wang*

傅大士

銘 *Ming*

The Mind King

by Master Fu (497-569)

The Mind King was written by Master Fu, a lay practitioner *(upasaka)* also known as Fu Yu, who lived during the reign of Emperor Wu Ti of the Liang dynasty. He married at the age of sixteen and had two sons. He started out as a fisherman, but later met an Indian monk and was moved to give up fishing and take up farming. It is not clear how he practiced or the circumstances under which he became enlightened. We know only that his enlightenment occurred while he was farming. He wrote a famous verse about the experience:

> *The empty hand holds the hoe.*
> *Feet walking, riding the water buffalo.*
> *The man walks over the bridge*
> *The bridge flows, the water does not flow.*

The Mind King describes the mind after enlightenment. It is not the rational mind of analysis or judgment; rather, this mind is the basis of all the Buddhas. If we

can understand this mind then we can really see that
we are also the Buddha. From the point of view of the
Buddha, neither mind nor form exists, but from the
perspective of the discriminating mind full of vexations, this mind is pure, and empty of desire and
aversion. Although sentient beings are attached to
desire and aversion, they have never really departed
from the pure mind. As soon as we let go of our
vexations, pure mind will manifest, and life will be
free and easy, as it was for the Buddha. Thus the mind
of vexation and the pure mind are fundamentally one
and the same. But to what extent can you put down
the mind of vexation? "If you put down one thought,
that will be one instance of Buddha mind. If you put
down all thoughts, then you will have continuous
Buddha mind." These two sentences come from a
Pure Land sutra entitled *Kuan Wu Liang Shou Fo Ching
(Sutra of Contemplation on the Buddha of Unlimited
Lives)*. Master Fu definitely belongs to the Ch'an
school, but his idea of the pure mind is also consistent
with the highest ideals of the Pure Land school.

The Mind King

Contemplate the mind; this king of emptiness
Is subtle and abstruse.
Without shape or form,
It has great spiritual power.

It can eliminate all calamities
And accomplish all merits.
Though its essence is empty,
It is the measure of dharmas.

When you look, it is formless;
When you call, it echoes.
It is the great Dharma commander,
Transmitting the sutras through precepts of mind.

As saltiness in sea water,
Transparency in color,
Surely it is there,
But its form is invisible;
The Mind King is also thus,
Residing in the body.

It comes in and out before your eyes,
Responding to phenomena, following emotions.
When it is carefree, without obstruction,
All endeavors are succesful.

When you realize original mind,
The mind sees Buddha.
This mind is Buddha;
This Buddha is mind.

Every thought is Buddha mind;
Buddha mind dwells on Buddha.
If you wish to accomplish this soon,
Be vigilant and disciplined.

Pure precepts purify the mind;
The mind then is Buddha.
Apart from this Mind King,
There is no other Buddha.

If you wish to seek Buddhahood,
Don't stain a single thing.
Though the nature of mind is empty,
Greed and hatred are real.

When you enter this Dharma door,
Sitting upright, you become Buddha.
Upon reaching the other shore,
You attain perfection.

True aspirants of the Tao
Contemplate their own mind.
Knowing Buddha lies within,
There is no need to search outside.

THE MIND KING

Right now mind is Buddha;
Right now Buddha is mind.
The shining mind knows the Buddha;
The enlightened one knows the mind.

Apart from mind, no Buddha;
Apart from Buddha, no mind.
Those who are not Buddha cannot penetrate;
They are not fit for the task.

Grasping emptiness and blocking tranquility
Results in floating and sinking.
No Buddhas or bodhisattvas
Settle their minds this way.

The Great Being of shining mind
Awakened to this subtle sound.
The nature of body and mind is wonderful;
Their functions need not be altered.

Thus the wise one
Puts the mind down and lets it be.
Don't say the Mind King
Is empty and without essence;
It can cause the body
To do evil and good.

It does not exist, nor is it nonexistent.
It appears and disappears unpredictably.

When the nature of mind departs from emptiness,
It can be sacred or profane.

Thus we urge one another
To guard it with care.
At the moment of fashioning,
It reverts to floating and sinking.

The wisdom of pure mind
Is as precious as gold.
The Dharma store of prajna
Is within body and mind.

The Dharma treasure of non-action
Is neither shallow nor deep.
All Buddhas and bodhisattvas
Have realized this original mind.
For those whose conditions are right,
It is neither past, present or future.

Faith in Mind

信 Hsin

心 Hsin

銘 Ming

三祖僧璨

Faith in Mind

by Seng Ts'an (?-606)

In the records of Ch'an masters, there is no full account of the life of Seng Ts'an, the Third Patriarch of
Ch'an, but we do know that the Fourth Patriarch, Tao
Hsin, served as his personal attendant for twelve
years. This can be taken as proof of Seng Ts'an's
existence, although it is not known where he was
from. Aside from the poem *Faith in Mind*, the only
written record of his teachings is on a stone tablet
commemorating him. The essence of the inscription is:
Simultaneously practice stillness *(chi)* and illumination *(chao)*. Carefully observe, but see no dharmas, see
no body and see no mind. For the mind is nameless,
the body is empty and the dharmas are a dream. There
is nothing to be attained, no enlightenment to be
experienced. This is called liberation.

 There is some doubt among scholars whether
Seng Ts'an was the author of *Faith in Mind*. Some
people suggest it was written after Niu T'ou Fa Jung's
Song of Mind in order to improve upon that poem.
With this question of attribution in mind, we will

assume for now that Seng Ts'an is the poet.

"Faith in mind" contains the two meanings of "believing in" and "realizing" the mind. The poem emphasizes the methods of practice. Seng Ts'an shows us how to transform our ordinary discriminating mind into the Buddha mind without discrimination; in other words, how to get from existence to emptiness, from defilement to purity. He tells us what kind of mental attitude we should avoid during the course of practice: we should not give in to our likes and dislikes, neither trying to get rid of our vexations nor seeking enlightenment. The practice is just for its own sake, and even though it has no other purpose, in the end the mind of equanimity *(ping deng hsin)* is realized; there is then no discrimination, and no need for language or, indeed, of practice.

The poem contains phrases that will later on become important in the Ts'ao Tung (Jap: Soto) sect, for instance "One thought for ten thousand years" *(i nien wan nien)*, which expresses the idea of one thought not moving and yet illuminating. This idea is to be the hallmark of Hung Chih Cheng Chueh's Silent Illumination Ch'an.

Faith in Mind

The Supreme Way is not difficult
If only you do not pick and choose.
Neither love nor hate,
And you will clearly understand.
Be off by a hair,
And you are as far apart as heaven from earth.
If you want it to appear,
Be neither for nor against.
For and against opposing each other —
This is the mind's disease.
Without recognizing the mysterious principle
It is useless to practice quietude.
The Way is perfect like great space,
Without lack, without excess.
Because of grasping and rejecting,
You cannot attain it.
Do not pursue conditioned existence;
Do not abide in acceptance of emptinesss.
In oneness and equality,
Confusion vanishes of itself.
Stop activity and return to stillness,
And that stillness will be even more active.
Only stagnating in duality,
How can you recognize oneness?
If you fail to penetrate oneness,
Both places lose their function.
Banish existence and you fall into existence;

Follow emptiness and you turn your back on it.
Excessive talking and thinking
Turn you from harmony with the Way.
Cut off talking and thinking,
And there is nowhere you cannot penetrate.
Return to the root and attain the principle;
Pursue illumination and you lose it.
One moment of reversing the light
Is greater than the previous emptiness.
The previous emptiness is transformed;
It was all a product of deluded views.
No need to seek the real;
Just extinguish your views.
Do not abide in dualistic views;
Take care not to seek after them.
As soon as there is right and wrong
The mind is scattered and lost.
Two comes from one,
Yet do not even keep the one.
When one mind does not arise,
Myriad dharmas are without defect.
Without defect, without dharmas,
No arising, no mind.
The subject is extinguished with the object.
The object sinks away with the subject.
Object is object because of the subject;
Subject is subject because of the object.
Know that the two
Are originally one emptiness.

In one emptiness the two are the same,
Containing all phenomena.
Not seeing fine or coarse,
How can there be any bias?
The Great Way is broad,
Neither easy nor difficult.
With narrow views and doubts,
Haste will slow you down.
Attach to it and you lose the measure;
The mind will enter a deviant path.
Let it go and be spontaneous,
Experience no going or staying.
Accord with your nature, unite with the Way,
Wander at ease, without vexation.
Bound by thoughts, you depart from the real;
And sinking into a stupor is as bad.
It is not good to weary the spirit.
Why alternate between aversion and affection?
If you wish to enter the one vehicle,
Do not be repelled by the sense realm.
With no aversion to the sense realm,
You become one with true enlightenment.
The wise have no motives;
Fools put themselves in bondage.
One dharma is not different from another.
The deluded mind clings to whatever it desires.
Using mind to cultivate mind —
Is this not a great mistake?
The erring mind begets tranquility and confusion;

In enlightenment there are no likes or dislikes.
The duality of all things
Issues from false discriminations.
A dream, an illusion, a flower in the sky —
How could they be worth grasping?
Gain and loss, right and wrong —
Discard them all at once.
If the eyes do not close in sleep,
All dreams will cease of themselves.
If the mind does not discriminate,
All dharmas are of one suchness.
The essence of one suchness is profound;
Unmoving, conditioned things are forgotton.
Contemplate all dharmas as equal,
And you return to things as they are.
When the subject disappears,
There can be no measuring or comparing.
Stop activity and there is no activity;
When activity stops, there is no rest.
Since two cannot be established,
How can there be one?
In the very ultimate,
Rules and standards do not exist.
Develop a mind of equanimity,
And all deeds are put to rest.
Anxious doubts are completely cleared.
Right faith is made upright.
Nothing lingers behind,
Nothing can be remembered.

Bright and empty, functioning naturally,
The mind does not exert itself.
It is not a place of thinking,
Difficult for reason and emotion to fathom.
In the Dharma Realm of true suchness,
There is no other, no self.
To accord with it is vitally important;
Only refer to "not-two."
In not-two all things are in unity;
Nothing is not included.
The wise throughout the ten directions
All enter this principle.
This principle is neither hurried nor slow —
One thought for ten thousand years.
Abiding nowhere yet everywhere,
The ten directions are right before you.
The smallest is the same as the largest
In the realm where delusion is cut off.
The largest is the same as the smallest;
No boundaries are visible.
Existence is precisely emptiness;
Emptiness is precisely existence.
If it is not like this,
Then you must not preserve it.
One is everything;
Everything is one.
If you can be like this,
Why worry about not finishing?
Faith and mind are not two;

Non-duality is faith in mind.
The path of words is cut off;
There is no past, no future, no present.

Song of Mind

心

Hsin

牛頭法融

銘

Ming

Song of Mind

by Niu T'ou Fa Jung (594-657)

Niu T'ou was a disciple of the Fourth Patriarch, Tao Hsin, and a Dharma brother of the Fifth Patriarch, Hung Jen. Since he left home with a scholarly master of the *San Lun* (Three Treatise) school, his early study consisted of theory. Moreover, he was very familiar with Confucian and Taoist philosophy and Chinese history. He was also knowledgeable in the arts of medicine and Taoist ritual. But he especially favored Ch'an meditation and practiced for twenty years deep in a mountain forest. Tao Hsin heard of Niu T'ou, and knowing that he had not yet achieved enlightenment, went to help him. After his enlightenment, Niu T'ou started out with 100 students, which later increased to 300. He often lectured on the Lotus and Prajnaparamita Sutras. His thought also included the Vimalakirti and Hua Yen (Avatamsaka) Sutras.

In *Song of Mind* Niu T'ou explains that our mind is originally pure, but if one thought enters, the purity vanishes. He puts great importance on a method of practice which is to watch our thoughts arising and disappearing. But the arising and disappearing (literally, birth and destruction) in our mind is really a kind of illusion, because if the previous thought remains unmoving and does not disappear, the later thought will not arise, nor can it be cut off. Thus both the Buddha and sentient beings originally have no mind. But in order for sentient beings to attain Buddhahood their illusory mind must be caused to become no-mind. Niu T'ou's method emphasizes using wakefulness *(hsing)* and stillness *(chi)* together. You should not attach to either of them. In the beginning, we still must rely on our sense organs to observe the world, but we should not let our discriminating mind attach to the world. If we let go of discrimination the world that is presented to our senses will disappear. Along with the vanishing of the world, our mind also vanishes. When you reach that point, you can still function normally in the world — in fact, others will still see you as an ordinary person. The only difference is that your mind is not moving, or in other words, not discriminating. Therefore, the *Song of Mind* says that right enlightenment is no enlightenment and true emptiness is not empty. Without leaving "emptiness" you can still spread the Dharma and even continue practicing. But this time you are not practicing to become a Buddha but because practice is just what you do. Ordinary people feel they must have a reason for doing something, but to practice with a goal in mind makes it impossible to get to the state of no-mind.

Song of Mind

The nature of mind is non-arising;
What need is there of knowledge and views?
Originally there is not a single dharma;
Why discuss inspiration and training?

Coming and going without beginning;
Sought for, it is not seen.
No need to do anything;
It is bright, still, self-apparent.

The past is like empty space;
Know anything and the basic principle is lost.
Casting a clear light on the world,
Illuminating, yet obscured.

If one-mindedness is impeded,
All dharmas are misunderstood.
Coming and going thus,
Is there need for thorough investigation?

Arising without the mark of arising,
Arising and illumination are the same.
Desiring to purify the mind,
There is no mind for effort.

Throughout time and space nothing is illuminated;
This is most profound.

Knowing dharmas is not knowing;
Not knowing is knowing the essential.

Using the mind to maintain quietude,
You still fail to leave the sickness.
Birth and death forgotten —
This is Original Nature.

The highest principle cannot be explained;
It is neither free nor bound.
Lively and attuned to everything,
It is always right before you.

There is nothing in front of you;
Nothing, yet everything is as usual.
Do not belabor wisdom to examine it;
Substance itself is empty and obscure.

Thoughts arise and pass away,
The preceding no different from the succeeding.
If the succeeding thought does not arise,
The preceding thought cuts itself off.

In past, present and future there is nothing;
No mind, no Buddha.
Sentient beings are without mind;
Out of no-mind, they manifest.

Distinguishing between profane and sacred,
Their vexations flourish.

SONG OF MIND

Splitting hairs deviates from the eternal.
Seeking the real, you give up the true.

Discarding both is the cure,
Transparent, bright, pure.
No need for hard work or skill;
Keep to the actions of an infant.

Alertly knowing,
The net of views abounds.
Stillness without seeing,
Not moving in a dark room.

Wakeful without wandering,
The mind is tranquil yet bright.
All phenomena are real and eternal,
Profuse, yet of a single form.

Going, coming, sitting, standing,
Don't attach to anything.
Affirming no direction,
Can there be leaving and entering?

There is neither unifying nor dispersing,
Neither slow nor quick.
Brightness and tranquility are just as they are;
They cannot be explained in words.

Mind is without alienation;
No need to terminate lust.

Nature being empty, lust will depart by itself.
Allow the mind to float and sink.

Neither clear nor clouded,
Neither shallow nor deep,
Originally it was not ancient;
At present it is not modern.

Now it is non-abiding;
Now it is Original Mind.
Originally it did not exist;
"Origin" is the present moment.

Bodhi has always existed;
No need to preserve it.
Vexation has never existed;
No need to eliminate it.

Natural wisdom is self-illuminating;
All dharmas return to thusness.
There is no returning, no receiving;
Stop contemplating, forget keeping.

The four virtues[1] are unborn;
The three bodies[2] have always existed.
The six sense organs contact their realms;
Discrimination is not consciousness.

In one-mindedness there are no wandering thoughts,
The myriad conditions harmonize.

SONG OF MIND

Mind and nature are originally alike;
Together, yet not mutually dependent.

Without arising, complying with phenomena,
Abiding hidden everywhere.
Enlightenment arises from non-enlightenment.
It is enlightening to non-enlightenment.

As to gain and loss,
Why call either good or bad?
Everything that is active
Originally was uncreated.

Know that mind is not mind;
There is no sickness, no medicine.
When in confusion, you must discard affairs;
Enlightened, it makes no difference.

Originally there is nothing to obtain;
Now what use is there in discarding?
When someone claims to see demons,
We may talk of emptiness, yet the phenomena
      are there.
Don't destroy the emotions of common people;
Only teach the cessation of thoughts.

When thoughts are gone, mind is abolished;
When mind is gone, action is terminated.
No need to confirm emptiness;
Naturally, there is clear comprehension.

Completely extinguishing birth and death,
The profound mind enters into principle.
Opening your eyes and seeing forms,
Mind arises in accord with the environment.

Within mind there is no environment;
Within the environment there is no mind.
Use mind to extinguish the environment
And both will be disturbed.

With mind still and environment thus,
Not discarding, not grasping,
Environment is extinguished together with mind.
Mind disappears together with environment.

When neither arise,
There is tranquility and limitless brightness.
The reflection of Bodhi appears
In the eternally clear water of mind.

The nature of merit is like a simpleton:
It does not establish closeness and distance.
Favor and disgrace do not change it;
It doesn't choose its abode.

All connections suddenly cease;
Everything is forgotten.
Eternal day is like night,
Eternal night, like day.

SONG OF MIND

Outwardly like a complete fool,
Inwardly mind is empty and real.
Those not moved by environment
Are strong and great.

There is neither people nor seeing;
Without seeing there is constant appearance.
Completely penetrating everything,
It has always pervaded everywhere.

Thinking brings unclarity,
Sinking and confusing the spirit.
Use mind to stop activity
And it becomes even more erratic.

The ten thousand dharmas are everywhere,
Yet there is only one door.
Neither entering nor leaving,
Neither quiet nor noisy.

The wisdom of sravakas and pratyekabuddhas[3]
Cannot explain it.
Actually there is not a single thing;
Only wonderful wisdom exists.

The original face is limitless;
It cannot be probed by mind.
True enlightenment is no enlightenment,
Real emptiness is not empty.

All Buddhas of the past, present and future
All ride on this basic principle.
The tip of a hair of this basic principle
Contains worlds numerous as the Ganges sands.

Do not concern yourself with anything;
Fix the mind nowhere.
Fixing the mind nowhere,
Limitless brightness shows itself.

Tranquil and non-arising,
Set free in boundless time and space.
Whatever it does, there is no obstruction;
Going and staying are equal.

The sun of wisdom is tranquil,
The light of samadhi is bright.
Illuminating the garden of no forms,
Shining on the city of Nirvana.

After all relationships are forgotten,
Spirit is understood and settled in substance.
Not rising from the Dharma seat,
Sleeping peacefully in a vacant room.

Taking pleasure in Tao is calming,
Wandering free and easy in reality.
No action and nothing to attain,
Relying on nothing, manifesting naturally.

The four unlimited minds[4] and the six paramitas[5]
Are all on the path of one vehicle.
If mind is not born,
Dharmas will not differ from one another.

Knowing arising is non-arising,
Eternity appears now.
Only the wise understand,
No words can explain enlightenment.

1. The four virtues (of Nirvana): permanence, bliss, self, purity.

2. The three-fold body of the Buddha: Dharmakaya, body of essential nature; Sambhogakaya, reward or enjoyment body; Nirmanakaya, transformation body.

3. Sravakas and pratyekabuddhas refer to disciples of the Hinayana path. Sravakas attain Nirvana by hearing the Buddha's doctrine, and pratyeka-buddhas become enlightened through their own contemplation of the twelve causes and conditions.

4. The four unlimited minds: kindness, pity, joy, equanimity (or protection).

5. The six paramitas, or perfections: giving, precepts, forbearance, diligence, meditation, wisdom.

Song of Enlightenment

證 Cheng

道 Tao

永嘉玄覺 歌 Ko

Song of Enlightenment

by Yung Chia Hsuan Chueh (665-713)

Already a monk at the age of eight, Yung Chia became
a very accomplished Buddhist scholar, and read just
about the entire Buddhist literature, especially concen-
trating on the T'ien T'ai school. He built a tiny hut and
retired there to practice, using the *chih-kuan (samatha-
vipasyana)* method of T'ien T'ai. Among Yung Chia's
works relating to this method are *Song of Samatha* and
Song of Vipasyana. Although his poems on Ch'an
practice show a T'ien T'ai influence, they cannot be
equated with T'ien T'ai works since he emphasizes
practice rather than the formal principles of T'ien T'ai.

    Song of Enlightenment was written after Yung Chia
had met with the Sixth Patriarch, Hui Neng. What
occurred at that meeting was very unusual. Yung
Chia was full of self-confidence, but he sought out
Hui Neng to obtain *yin-k'o,* or certification, of his level
of attainment. When he saw the Sixth Patriarch, he did
not bow or show any outward gesture of respect. Hui
Neng thought it was odd that a monk should exhibit
such arrogance and asked him about it. Yung Chia

replied, "The matter of life and death is more important because impermanence is too brief." Hui Neng asked, "But why can't you experience no-birth and why can't you realize no-speed?" No-birth refers to the non-moving of time and no-speed refers to the non-moving of space. Yung Chia answered, "Experience is originally no-birth and realization is originally no-speed." Hui Neng said, "That's right." Then Yung Chia bowed very reverently to Hui Neng. Yung Chia was already enlightened, but he needed Hui Neng's confirmation to secure his faith. Having reached his objective, he quickly turned to leave. But Hui Neng stopped him, saying, "Since you already understand the meaning of no-birth, why be in such a hurry?", thus indirectly asking Yung Chia to stay with him. Yung Chia only saw Hui Neng this once and spent one night at his place, but he was nevertheless a very special disciple of the Sixth Patriarch. Yung Chia died at the age of forty-nine, and we have no idea of how many disciples he had.

In the title of this poem, *cheng tao* can mean both "experience of enlightenment" or "proving the Way." The important point of the *Song of Enlightenment* is revealed in the beginning of the poem — that ignorance is the Buddha nature and the illusory body is the Dharma Body. The poem also says that the five *skandhas* are like the coming and going of floating clouds and the three poisons are like the appearing and disappearing of water bubbles. The Buddha Way, or Ch'an, does not depart from the normal, phenom-

enal world even though Buddhism sees it as illusory.
From the point of view of the enlightened person, it is
just floating clouds and water bubbles but to an
ordinary person, it is real; this is what makes them
ordinary people with vexations.

What is the Tao, or the Buddha Way? Tao has a
dual meaning: the "way" to achieve Buddhahood —
the practice, and the Way of the Buddhas — the actual
attainment of Buddhahood. Yung Chia describes both
the practice and the situation after realization. Yung
Chia's teachings on practice follow those of the Sixth
Patriarch — that walking, sitting and all other activity
are just Ch'an; and that there is a need to have a
thorough understanding of both the basic principles
and the teaching of Ch'an. He also advises the practitioner to ignore praise or blame from others and just
concentrate on the practice of the "formless Dharma."
It is important not to make the theoretical teaching our
goal. The practice should not be to show that you are
a practitioner or to reach any particular goal; the
practice itself is the goal. The enlightened person "will
clearly see that nothing exists; there is neither person
nor Buddha." The faith of an enlightened one is such
that it cannot be shaken even in the face of danger.
This realization of the Way cannot be destroyed by
anyone or anything.

Song of Enlightenment

Have you not seen the idle man of Tao who has
    nothing to learn and nothing to do,
Who neither discards wandering thoughts nor seeks
    the truth?
The real nature of ignorance is Buddha-nature;
The illusory empty body is the Dharma body.

After realizing the Dharma body, there is not a thing;
Original self-nature is the innate Buddha.
The five skandhas[1] — the empty comings and goings of
    floating clouds;
The three poisons[2] — the vacant appearing and disap-
    pearing of water bubbles.

When the real is experienced, there is neither person
    nor dharma.
In an instant the Avici karma[3] is destroyed.
If I lie to deceive sentient beings,
May my tongue be ripped out for kalpas uncountable
    as dust and sand.

Suddenly enlightened to Tathagata Ch'an,
The six paramitas and myriad means are complete
    within that essence.
In dreams there are clearly six paths[4] of sentient beings;
Upon awakening the great chiliocosm[5] is completely
    empty.

There is no sin or merit, no loss or gain.
Don't look for anything in this Nirvanic nature;
Originally a dusty mirror which has never been
      polished,
Today it must be taken apart and analyzed.

Who has no thoughts? Who has no births?
If the unborn is real, there is nothing not born.
Ask the mechanical wooden puppet
When it will attain Buddhahood through practice.

Put down the four elements, don't cling to anything;
In this Nirvanic nature, feel free to eat and drink.
All phenomena are impermanent; all are empty.
This is the complete enlightenment of the Tathagata.

Surely this is the true vehicle.
One who disagrees is swayed by emotion.
Going directly to the root is the seal of the Buddha;
No point searching for branches or plucking leaves.

The mani pearl[6] is unknown to people;
It can be personally found in the Tathagatagarbha.[7]
The functions of the six senses are both empty and not
      empty,
One perfect light with form yet formless.

Purify the five eyes[8] to achieve the five powers.[9]
Only after realization can one comprehend.

SONG OF ENLIGHTENMENT

To see the image in a mirror is not difficult.
How can one grasp the moon in the water?

Always acting alone, walking alone,
Together the enlightened travel the Nirvana road.
The tune is ancient, the spirit pure, the style poised,
The face drawn, the bones hardened; people take no
    notice.

The penniless Buddhist monks say they are destitute;
Though they have nothing, they are not poor in Tao.
Poverty shows in the ragged robes they always wear.
The priceless treasures of the Tao are stored in their
    minds.

These priceless treasures have endless functions;
There is no hesitation in helping others.
The three bodies and four wisdoms[10] are complete in
    essence;
The eight liberations[11] and six psychic powers[12] are the
    mind-ground seal.

For the great ones, one breakthrough accomplishes all;
For the middling and inferior, the more they hear, the
    less they believe.
You only have to discard the dirty garments within;
No need to flaunt your diligence to others.

When criticized by others, let them wrong you;
They will tire themselves trying to burn the sky with a
    torch.
When I hear abuse, it is like drinking ambrosia;
Melt it and suddenly one enters the inconceivable.

If we regard criticism as merit,
The critics will become reliable friends.
Do not hate those who slander you;
How else can you manifest the unborn power of
    compassion?

Thoroughly understanding both basic principle and
    teaching,
Samadhi and wisdom are complete and clear without
    stagnating in emptiness.
Not only do I accomplish this now;
The essence of uncountable Buddhas is just the same.

Speak without fear as the lion roars;
All animals hearing it cringe in fright.
Losing his composure, the fragrant elephant gallops;
With quiet joy, the heavenly dragon listens.

Travelling over river, ocean and mountain stream,
Seeking teachers, asking of the way to investigate
    Ch'an,
Since I recognize the path of Ts'ao Ch'i,[13]
I realize all those do not relate to birth and death.

SONG OF ENLIGHTENMENT

Walking is Ch'an; sitting is Ch'an;
Speaking or silent, moving or still, the essence is
    undisturbed.
Remain composed even if facing a sharp weapon,
Be at ease even if given poison.
My teacher only met Dipankara Buddha[14]
After training in forbearance for many kalpas.

Continuing rounds of birth and death,
Samsara prolonged without interruption;
Since sudden enlightenment I understand the unborn.
Thus I have no concern for honor or shame.

Living in a hermitage deep in the mountains,
On a lonely peak under a dense pine tree,
I would meditate contentedly in a monk's hut,
At ease in this tranquil place.

After enlightenment no need for further effort;
All dharmas of activity are varied.
Giving alms with attachment bestows merit for
    heavenly birth,
Like shooting an arrow into space.

Once its power is expended, the arrow falls,
Bringing discontent in the next life.
How can this compare to the true door of non-action,
Through which one leaps straight into the Tathagata
    ground?

Once you get to the root, don't worry about the
    branches,
Like pure crystal containing a precious moon.
Since you have realized this all-giving pearl,
Benefit for yourself and others will never end.

The moon shines on the river, the breeze stirs the pine,
What is there to do on a long pleasant night?
Buddha-nature and the precepts jewel are sealed in
    the mind-ground.
Fog, dew and rosy clouds are now my garments.

The dragon-subduing alms bowl[15] and the staff that
    separates tigers,[16]
With the jangling of its two metal rings,
Are not outer forms of keeping the precepts,
But are holding the Tathagata's staff and treading his
    path.

Not seeking the true, nor rejecting the false,
Realize that both are empty and formless.
There is no form, no emptiness and no non-emptiness;
This is the true mark of the Tathagata.

The mirror of mind reflects without interference;
Its vastness and clarity radiate through countless
    worlds.
Various phenomena all manifest themselves;
To a perfectly illumined one there is neither inside nor
    outside.

Attaching to emptiness, denying cause and effect,
Brings calamities beyond measure.
Rejecting existence and grasping emptiness is the same
    mistake,
Like jumping into a fire to avoid drowning.

If you discard the illusory mind and grasp the true
    principle,
This mind of grasping and discarding becomes clever.
Not understanding this, practitioners engage in cultiva-
    tion,
Just as one mistakes a thief for his own son.

Loss of Dharma wealth and extinction of merits,
All are caused by the mind consciousness.
Through the Ch'an door, understand the cutting off of
    mind,
And suddenly enter the powerful view of the unborn.

The great hero uses the sword of wisdom;
This prajna blade blazes like a diamond.
It not only destroys the mind of the outer paths,
But long ago frightened away the heavenly demons.

Sound the Dharma thunder; beat the Dharma drum;
Spread the clouds of compassion and scatter ambrosia.
Where the elephant king treads the favors are boundless,
The three vehicles[17] and five natures[18] are awakened.

THE POETRY OF ENLIGHTENMENT

The pinodhi grass[19] in the snow mountains is un-
    mixed;
I often enjoy the pure ghee it produces.

One nature perfectly pervades all natures;
One Dharma includes all dharmas.
One moon appears in all waters;
The moons reflected in all waters are one.

The Dharma body of all Buddhas enters my nature;
Which is the same as the Tathagata's.
One stage encompasses all stages,
Not form nor mind nor karmic act.

Eighty thousand doors are completed in a snap of the
        fingers,
In a flash three kalpas are extinguished.
What do numbers, expressions, and their negations
Have to do with my spiritual awakening?

It is not perishable and cannot be praised,
Its substance is like limitless space.
Without leaving where it is, it is constantly clear.
When seeking, you know it cannot be found.
It cannot be grasped, nor can it be discarded;
It is obtained only in the unobtainable.

Speaking in silence, silent in speech,
The door of giving is wide open without obstruction.

SONG OF ENLIGHTENMENT

If someone asks what basic principle I interpret,
I will say it is the power of Mahaprajna.

Others don't know whether I am right or wrong,
Even devas cannot fathom whether I oppose or agree.
I have practiced for many kalpas;
I am not deceiving you as some idlers do.

Setting up the Dharma banner, establishing the basic
     principle,
Ts'ao Ch'i clearly followed the Buddha's decree.
The first one to pass on the lamp was Mahakasyapa;
In India it was transmitted through twenty-eight
     generations.

The Dharma flowed east and entered this land[20]
Where Bodhidharma was the First Patriarch.
Six generations transmitted the robe, as heard
     throughout the land,
And those who later attained the Tao cannot be
     counted.

The truth does not stand, the false is originally empty.
When both existence and non-existence are swept
     away, not empty is empty.
The twenty empty doors teach non-attachment.
The nature of all Tathagatas is one; their substance is
     the same.

The mind is a sense organ; dharmas are its object.
The two are like marks on a mirror.
Once the dust is rubbed off, the light begins to appear.
When both mind and dharmas are forgotten, this is
    true nature.

Oh, in this evil world in the Dharma-ending age,
Sentient beings have little fortune and are hard to
    discipline.
Far away from the time of the sages, perverted views
    run deep.
When demons are strong and Dharma is weak, fears
    and dangers abound.
When they hear the teaching of sudden enlightenment
    of the Tathagata,
They cannot but want to destroy it, to smash the tiles.

That which acts is the mind, that which receives
    retribution is the body;
No need to put the blame on others.
If you want to escape continuous karma,
Do not slander the Tathagata's wheel of right Dharma.

There are no other trees in a sandalwood forest.
The lion lives in luxuriant dense thickets.
He strolls along in the quiet woods,
All other animals and birds keep their distance.

A crowd of animals follows the lions's son,
Who can roar at the age of three.

SONG OF ENLIGHTENMENT

If a wild fox challenges the Dharma King,
It is like a monster opening his mouth for a hundred
    years.

The teaching of complete sudden enlightenment is not
    to be used as a favor.
All unsettled doubts must be debated until clear.
Not that I, a mountain monk, want to be presumptuous,
But cultivation may make you fall into the pit of cessa-
    tion and permanence.

Wrong is not wrong; right is not right;
The slightest deviation veers a thousand miles off
    course.
If right, the dragon maiden[21] becomes Buddha at once;
If wrong, the monk Suraksatra[22] falls alive into hell.

Since an early age I have accumulated knowledge,
Studying the sutras, shastras, and commentaries.
Discriminating between names and forms without rest,
I only troubled myself counting the sands in the sea.

I was severely reproached by the Tathagata:
What is the benefit of counting others' treasures?
I realized the futility of my dawdlings;
For many years I busied myself in the world in vain.

With evil capacity and mistaken understanding
One cannot penetrate the Tathagata's principle of
    complete sudden enlightenment.

Hinayana monks, though diligent, forget the mind of
Tao.
Outer path practitioners may be clever, but they lack
wisdom.

The ignorant and the foolish think
That the fist exists separately from the pointing finger.
Mistaking the finger for the moon, they practice
uselessly;
They only fabricate strange illusions in the realms of
sense and object.
Not perceiving a single dharma: this is Tathagata.
Only then can one be called the Supreme Observer.[23]

With this realization karmic obstacles are innately
empty.
Without realization, past debts must be paid off.
If one is unable to take the royal feast even when
hungry,
How can he be healed even if he meets the king of
doctors?

Practicing Ch'an in the desire realm[24] manifests the
power of knowledge,
Indestructible as a lotus grown in a fire.
Though Pradhanasura[25] broke the main precepts, he
awakened to the unborn;
He long ago reached the Buddha state and remains
there still.

Even when one preaches fearlessly as the lion roars,
The minds of the perverse and obstinate only harden.
They continue to break the main precepts and obstruct
    Bodhi
And cannot see the secret the Tathagata reveals.

Two monks broke the precepts against licentiousness
    and killing.
With his shallow knowledge, Upali[26] exaggerated the
    sin.
The great Vimalakirti[27] instantly removed their
    doubts,
Like a hot sun that melts ice and snow.

The power of the liberated is inconceivable,
With wonderful functions more numerous than the
    Ganges sands.
They would not refuse to make the four offerings[28]
To one who can accept ten thousand ounces of gold.
To have body broken and bones reduced to dust is not
    enough to repay
The words that enlighten, transcending countless
    eons.

The king in Dharma is the most superior;
The realization of countless Tathagatas are all alike.
Now I show you this all-giving pearl;
Believers are all in accord (with Dharma).

They clearly see that there is not a thing,
Neither person nor Buddha.
The numerous worlds in the great chiliocosm are
    bubbles in the sea,
All sages and saints are like lightning flashes.
Even if an iron wheel whirls on your head
Perfect, clear samadhi and wisdom are never lost.

The sun may turn cold and the moon may turn hot,
But the demons cannot destroy the true teaching.
When an elephant marches gloriously forward,
How can a praying mantis bar its way?

The elephant does not follow the rabbit's path;
The enlightened are not bound by trivial restraints.
Do not slander heaven when you observe it through a
    reed,
For those who do not yet know, I am giving you the
    key.

SONG OF ENLIGHTENMENT

1. The five skandhas, or aggregates of human existence: form, sensation, perception, volition and consciousness.

2. The three poisons: greed, hatred and ignorance.

3. Avici karma: retribution for any of the five unpardonable sins by rebirth in the Avici hell, one of the eight hot hells, in which suffering continues without interruption.

4. The six paths, or realms of rebirth for sentient beings: hell beings, pretas (hungry ghosts), animals, asuras (titans), humans and devas.

5. A great chiliocosm consists of 1,000,000,000 worlds.

6. Mani pearl: symbol of purity, of Buddha and his doctrine; also referred to as the all-giving pearl, or Cintamani.

7. Tathagatagarbha: womb, or store of the Tathagata — the potentiality of Buddhahood in each sentient being.

8. The five eyes: human, deva, wisdom, Dharma and Buddha.

9. The five powers: faith, diligence, mindfulness, samadhi and wisdom.

10. The four wisdoms of a Buddha: great mirror wisdom, wisdom of equality, subtle observing wisdom and perfecting wisdom.

11. The eight liberations, resulting from eight stages of meditation: 1) liberation arising from meditation on impurity, with attachment to form; 2) same as the first, without attachment to form; 3) liberation from desire by meditation on purity; 4) liberation in the state of boundless space; 5) liberation in the state of boundless consciousness; 6) liberation in the state of nothingness; 7) liberation in the state of neither thought nor absence of thought; 8) liberation in which there is extinction of sensation and perception.

12. The six psychic powers are: divine sight, divine hearing, knowledge of others' thoughts, knowledge of the former lives of self and others, power to appear anywhere at will, and insight into destruction of the asravas, or outflows.

13. Ts'ao Ch'i is another name for Hui Neng, the Sixth Patriarch; from a stream southeast of Shao-Chou in Kwangtung.

14. The teacher referred to here is Sakyamuni Buddha. Dipankara was the twenty-fourth predecessor of Sakyamuni; he predicted the latter's future Buddhahood during Sakyamuni's incarnation as Ju-t'ung Bodhisattva.

15. The dragon-subduing alms bowl refers to an incident when the Buddha compelled a naga to enter his alms bowl.

16. Reference to a story about a Ch'an master who separated two fighting tigers with his staff.

17. The three vehicles, or conveyances, which carry living beings across the sea of Samsara to the shore of Nirvana: Sravaka, Pratyekabuddha, and Bodhisattva.

18. The five natures, according to the Sutra of Complete Enlightenment, are: ordinary people, Hinayana, bodhisattvas, indefinite, and heterodox.

19. Pinodhi: a grass or herb said to enrich the milk of cattle.

20. The land referred to here is China, or the Middle Kingdom.

21. Nagakanya, the daughter of the dragon king at the bottom of the ocean, though female and a child of eight, instantly became a Buddha under the tutelage of Manjusri.

22. Suraksatra was a highly accomplished monk who studied the sutras deeply. Nevertheless, he slandered the Buddha's teachings and, as a result, was swallowed alive by the earth and fell into burning hell.

23. Another name for Avalokitesvara, or Observer of the World's Sounds.

24. The desire realm consists of the five lower paths of sentient beings plus the six heavens of desire.

25. A bodhisattva now in Sakyamuni's retinue.

26. Upali was a barber of the untouchable caste who
    became a disciple of Sakyamuni; he was one of the
    three most respected elders of the first Buddhist
    council, known as the authority on and compiler of
    the Vinaya.

27. Vimalakirti, a native of Vaisali and said to have been
    a contemporary of Sakyamuni, is the protagonist of a
    sutra bearing his name which promotes the
    Mahayana ideal of non-duality.

28. The four offerings, or provisions for a monk: cloth-
    ing, food, bedding (or dwelling), and medicine.

Inquiry into Matching Halves

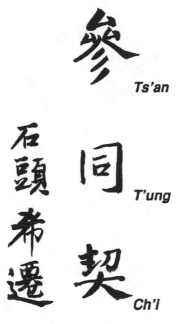

Ts'an

T'ung

Ch'i

Inquiry into Matching Halves

by Shih T'ou Hsi Ch'ien (700-790)

When Shih T'ou was a young novice he was a disciple
of Hui Neng. But after the Sixth Patriarch passed
away, he went to study with a master by the name of
Ch'ing Yuan Hsing Szu. There is a very amusing
anecdote concerning this. When Hui Neng was about
to die, Shih T'ou asked him what he should do and
Hui Neng answered that he should go to Hsing Szu.
Shih T'ou, unaware that there existed a master by that
name, thought he had been advised to "seek
thoughts" *(hsun szu)*. Thereafter he spent all his time
in quiet, isolated places practicing meditation, using
the method of watching his thoughts, until an elder
monk informed him that he had mistaken the term
hsun szu for the name Hsing Szu. Once, after he
became enlightened, he read an essay in Seng Chao's
Chao Lun called *Wu Pu Ch'ien Lun* (Things Not Moving), in which it is written: "If you take all things as
yourself, won't you be a sage?" When Shih T'ou read
this line he was inspired to write the poem *Ts'an T'ung
chi* or *Inquiry into Matching Halves*.

Ts'an means to "inquire into" or to "work on" and *t'ung ch'i*, which literally means "matching halves," can also be interpreted as "the mind-seal common to all Buddhas." Shih T'ou, who has already discovered the Buddha mind, is encouraging those who haven't to find out what it is through practice. The method he describes relates to the *I Ching*. In the Han dynasty (206 B.C. - A.D. 220), the Taoist scholar and master Wei Po Yang wrote a book also entitled *Ts'an T'ung Ch'i*, in which he uses the diagrams of the *I Ching* to show how to cultivate immortality. Shih T'ou used the same title because he wanted to draw a parallel: the Taoist book teaches the way to immortality by cultivating elixir; his poem teaches the way to Buddahood by cultivating Ch'an. Although based on Ch'an, the poem is influenced by Taoist and Confucian thought, as well as by Buddhist theory. For instance, the mention of brightness and darkness corresponds to the concepts of Yin and Yang in the *I Ching*. But even though he borrows the devices of Taoism, he uses them in a different context. Here, brightness indicates wisdom and darkness indicates vexation. As a result of incorporating ideas from other traditions of thought, Shih T'ou's expression of the style of practice does not resemble that of the Lin Chi sect, or most other sects of Ch'an. Later, when the Ts'ao Tung sect appeared, it was largely influenced by the thought of Shih T'ou as expressed in this poem.

This is a very difficult poem to understand due to its strong theoretical background. On the surface much of it seems obscure. Shih T'ou's purpose is to guide students in the practice, but his approach is philosophical. *Inquiry into Matching Halves* is rarely lectured on, because it requires familiarity with the background of Shih T'ou's thought, as well as a solid basis in Ch'an practice. An important key to Shih T'ou's thought is the concept of the mutual interaction *(hui hu)* of brightness and darkness. This means that the worlds of vexation and purity exist interdependently. If you leave one, then you leave the other. Becoming a Buddha, one does not depart from sentient beings, and sentient beings do not depart from the Buddha. He also emphasizes equanimity — not attaching to vexation or wisdom. To the unenlightened these things may be difficult to see clearly.

Inquiry into Matching Halves

The mind of the great Indian immortal
Was esoterically transmitted from West to East.
The capacity of people may be dull or sharp,
But there are no Northern and Southern patriarchs in
    the Tao.
The spiritual source is bright and pure,
Branching out and in darkness flowing forth.
Attachment to phenomena has always been confu-
    sion,
Yet union with principle is not enlightenment.
Every (Dharma) door includes all realms,
Some mutually interact, others don't.
Reaction increases mutual involvement;
There should be no reliance on abiding in one place.
From original form come shapes and images;
From primal sound come pleasures and pains.
In obscurity, words of the high and middle (paths) are
    in accord;
In lucidity, purity or muddiness of expression are
    apparent.
The four great elements return to their nature
As a child finds its mother.
Fire burns, wind moves and shakes,
Water moistens, earth solidifies.
Eyes — forms, ears — sounds,
Nose — smells, tongue — salty and sour.
In accordance with each dharma,

The root gives rise to separate leaves.
Root and branches must return to basic principle;
"Honorable" and "lowly" are merely words.
In the midst of brightness there is darkness;
Don't take darkness as darkness.
In the midst of darkness there is brightness;
Don't take brightness as brightness.
Brightness and darkness correspond,
Like one step following another.
All things have their own function
Depending on their use and location.
Phenomena store, seal, cover, combine.
Principle yields to the arrow, the sword's edge, the
    stick.
Received teachings must be reconciled with basic
    principle;
Do not establish your own rules.
Using your eyes, the path is lost;
Using your feet, how can you know the road?
Moving forward there is no near or far;
Confusion creates mountains and rivers of obstruc-
    tions.
I implore those who investigate the mysterious:
Do not waste your time!

Song of the
Precious Mirror Samadhi

寶　Pao

鏡　Ching

三　San

昧　Mei

歌　Ko

洞山良价

Song of the Precious Mirror Samadhi

by Tung Shan Liang Chieh (807-869)

Tung Shan, the founder of the Ts'ao Tung school, was
the fourth generation in the line of Shih T'ou Hsi
Ch'ien. He left home at an early age. One day he
asked his teacher, Master Yun Yen, "Someone once
said that non-sentient beings could speak the Dharma.
If so, who can hear it?" Yun Yen said, "When non-
sentient beings speak the Dharma, non-sentient beings
hear it." Tung Shan then asked again, "Master, do you
hear it?" Yun Yen replied, "If I were able to hear it,
then you would not be able to hear my speech." Tung
Shan retorted, "But Master, I don't hear the Dharma
you are speaking!" Yun Yen said, "You can't even
hear the Dharma I am speaking, and still you want to
hear the Dharma that non-sentient beings are speaking?" Tung Shan thought this was all very strange. He
said to himself: "If I can't hear it with my ears, maybe
I should use my eyes to hear it." Then he left Master
Yun Yen and went traveling. But this big question
stuck in his mind. One day as he was wading across a
river he looked down and saw his reflection in the
water. At that point he understood the conversation

that passed between Master Yun Yen and himself.

In the title of this poem, "precious" can be interpreted as eternal, unchanging and limitless. The characteristic of the mirror is its brightness; it can shine inwardly to enlighten you to your own nature, or it can shine outwardly to enable you to help others. "Samadhi" here refers to the enlightened state, the mind of Ch'an.

The central image of the poem is an infant who is born complete with all five sense organs. This signifies that an unenlightened person is originally equipped with the same characteristics as a Buddha. Prior to Tung Shan, the Ch'an school was generally characterized by its emphasis on sudden enlightenment, without any levels. But he tried to discern the various levels of his students and used a five-stage scheme to test their accomplishments. Although these five levels are distinct, they all have the same basis in enlightenment; thus it cannot be said that a student on a deeper level is enlightened while one on a shallower level is not. The five levels, arising from a single center, interact with each other. This concept of mutual interaction *(hui-hu)* shows Tung Shan's relationship to Shih T'ou Hsi Ch'ien, his great-grandmaster. To illustrate the concept, Tung Shan makes use of the Yin and Yang lines of the I Ching, especially the Li trigram which he combines into five formations. But Tung Shan's primary purpose is not to propagate the I Ching but rather to help people in the practice of Ch'an.

Song of the Precious Mirror Samadhi

It is this very Dharma
The Buddha and Patriarchs secretly transmitted.
Now that you have it
Protect it well.

Like a silver bowl full of snow
Or an egret hidden against the bright moon
They are similar but not identical.
When mingled their difference can be recognized.

The meaning does not lie in words,
Yet those who are ripe must be taught.
As soon as you act it is a dead issue,
So consider their varying attainments.

Rejecting words or clinging to them are both mistakes,
Like a blazing fire, useful but dangerous.
If it is only expressed in language
The precious mirror will be stained.

At midnight it is truly bright;
By daybreak it no longer shows.
It serves as the law which governs all things;
Use it to uproot all suffering.

Though it is not a way of action
Still, it is not without words.

As before a precious mirror,
The form and reflection gaze on each other —
You are not it,
But it is just you.

Just as an infant
Is equipped with five sense organs,
It neither goes nor comes,
Neither does it arise or abide.

"P'o-p'o H'o-h'o"[1] —
A phrase, but without meaning.
You can never get the substance of it
Because it is not correct language.

Doubling the Li trigram[2] makes six lines.
The outer and inner lines mutually interact.
Stacked, they become three pairs;
At most they can transform into five.

Like the (five) aromas of the hyssop plant
Or (the five branches of) the vajra sceptre
The exact center subtly harmonizing,
Drumming and singing simultaneously.

Penetrate the goal and you will fathom the way.
In order to lead there must be a road.
To be wrong is auspicious;
Do not oppose it.

SONG OF THE PRECIOUS MIRROR SAMADHI

Natural and subtle,
It is neither ignorance nor enlightenment.
Causes and conditions have their time and season,
Tranquil and illuminating.

It is so small it enters the spaceless,
So large it is beyond dimension.
If you are off by a hair's breadth
Then you would be out of harmony.

Now there is sudden and gradual (enlightenment)
In order to establish the fundamental guidelines.
When the fundamental guidelines are clear
It becomes the rule.

Realization of the basic principle is the ultimate
     standard,
Genuine, constant, yet flowing,
With still body but racing mind,
Like a tethered horse or a mouse frozen by fright.

Past sages pitied them
And liberated them with Buddha Dharma.
Following their upside-down ways
They took black for white.
When inverted thinking disappears,
They realize Mind of their own accord.

If you want to merge with the ancient track
Then contemplate the ancients.

At the completion of the Buddha Path
Ten kalpas of contemplation will be established.

Like a tiger's lame foot,
Like a shoeless horse,
Because there is a defect
They seek the jewelled bench and the priceless halter.
Because you are astonished
You realize you were like the brown or white ox.

Hou-i[3] used his skill
To hit the target at a hundred paces.
As soon as the arrow hits the mark
Of what further use is his skill?

When a wooden man breaks into song,
A stone woman gets up to dance.
Since this cannot be understood by reasoning
How can it be analyzed?

The minister serves his lord;
The son obeys his father.
If he does not obey, he is not filial;
If the minister does not serve, he is not loyal.

To cultivate in hiding, functioning in secret,
Like a fool, like a dolt;
If only you are able to persist,
You will be called a master among masters.

1. This phrase is used to describe an infant's uttering.

2. Li is the third trigram of the I Ching: ☲

3. A famous archer.

Silent Illumination

黙
Mo

宏　照
智　　　Chao
正
覺　銘
　　　Ming

Silent Illumination

by Hung Chih Cheng Chueh (1091-1157)

The major methods of Ch'an, which have survived to
the present day, are the Kung-an method, associated
with the Lin Chi (Jap: Rinzai) sect, and Silent Illumination, associated with the Ts'ao Tung (Jap: Soto) sect.
Hung Chih Cheng Chueh, the greatest advocate of
Silent Illumination, is often contrasted with his
contemporary, Ta Hui Tsung Kao, the greatest advocate of the use of kung-ans.

   Hung Chih, a native of Shansi, became a monk at
the age of eleven. During a pilgrimage in Honan,
when he was eighteen, he met K'u Mu Fa Ch'eng, a
Ts'ao Tung master. He attained some realization
under K'u Mu but was only thoroughly enlightened at
twenty-three under K'u Mu's Dharma brother, Master
Tan Hsia Tzu Ch'un. Hung Chih considered the ideas
of Shih T'ou and Tung Shan, such as mutual interaction, equanimity, and the non-duality of phenomena
and principle, as the ultimate teachings of Mahayana.
But his style of practice was most influenced by his
teacher K'u Mu (dry wood), so-named because when
he sat, his stillness made his body resemble a block of

dry wood. Hung Chih, calling his method "Silent Illumination," describes it as follows: "Your body sits silently; your mind, quiescent, unmoving. Your mouth is so still that moss grows around it. Grass sprouts from your tongue. Do this without cease, cleansing the mind until it gains the clarity of an autumn pool, bright as the moon illuminating the evening sky."

Hung Chih also said, "In this silent sitting, whatever realms may appear, the mind is very clear as to all the details, yet everything is where it originally is, in its own place. The mind stays on one thought for ten thousand years, yet does not dwell on any forms, inside or outside." This teaching of Hung Chih reveals the aim of Silent Illumination: a mind unburdened with thoughts yet profoundly aware of its own state. Both silence and illumination must be present. Later, after returning from study with Ch'an masters in China, Master Dogen (1200-1253) introduced a similar teaching to Japan, called *Shikantaza.*

Silent Illumination

Silently and serenely, one forgets all words,
Clearly and vividly, it appears before you.
When one realizes it, time has no limits.
When experienced, your surroundings come to life.
Singularly illuminating is this bright awareness,
Full of wonder is the pure illumination.
The moon's appearance, a river of stars,
Snow-clad pines, clouds hovering on mountain peaks.
In darkness, they glow with brightness.
In shadows, they shine with a splendid light.
Like the dreaming of a crane flying in empty space,
Like the clear, still water of an autumn pool,
Endless eons dissolve into nothingness,
Each indistinguishable from the other.
In this illumination all striving is forgotten.
Where does this wonder exist?
Brightness and clarity dispel confusion
On the path of Silent Illumination,
The origin of the infinitesimal.
To penetrate the extremely small,
There is the gold shuttle on a loom of jade.
Subject and object influence each other.
Light and darkness are mutually dependent.
There is neither mind nor world to rely on,
Yet do the two interact, mutually.
Drink the medicine of correct views.
Beat the poison-smeared drum.

When silence and illumination are complete
Killing and bringing to life are choices I make.
At last, through the door, one emerges.
The fruit has ripened on the branch.
Only this Silence is the ultimate teaching.
Only this Illumination, the universal response.
The response is without effort.
The teaching, not heard with the ears.
Throughout the universe, all things
Emit light and speak the Dharma.
They testify to each other,
Answering each other's questions.
Mutually answering and testifying,
Responding in perfect harmony.
When illumination is without serenity,
Then will distinctions be seen.
Mutually testifying and answering,
Giving rise to disharmony.
If within serenity illumination is lost,
All will become wasteful and secondary.
When Silent Illumination is complete,
The lotus will blossom, the dreamer will awaken.
The hundred rivers flow to the ocean,
The thousand mountains face the loftiest peak.
Like the goose preferring milk to water,
Like a busy bee gathering pollen,
When Silent Illumination reaches the ultimate,
I carry on the original tradition of my sect.
This practice is called Silent Illumination.
It penetrates from the deepest to the highest.

On Clear Mind

Contemplating Mind

觀 *Ch'eng* 澄 *Kuan*

憨 心 *Hsin* 心 *Hsin*

山

德 銘 *Ming* 銘 *Ming*

清

On Clear Mind
Contemplating Mind

by Han Shan Te Ch'ing (1546-1623)

Han Shan was a great Ch'an practitioner, scholar and
writer who lived at the close of the Ming dynasty. His
autobiography, which includes a detailed account of
his practice and enlightenment, has been translated
into English by Charles Luk and published in *Practical
Buddhism*. (This Han Shan should not be confused
with another poet of the same phonetic name, who is
known in the West as Cold Mountain.) At the age of
seven Han Shan was already grappling with the great
questions of origin and destiny. At nine he left the
home life, finally becoming a monk at nineteen. Han
Shan had many enlightenment experiences. In one of
his deeper experiences, he suddenly entered a state of
samadhi while taking a walk and saw a brilliant light
like a huge, perfect mirror, with everything in the
world reflected in it. Upon returning from samadhi,
his body and mind were completely clear; he realized
there was nothing to attain:

In the flash of one thought
My turbulent mind came to a rest.
The inner and the outer,
The senses and their objects,
Are thoroughly lucid.
In a complete turnabout
I smashed the Great Emptiness.
The ten thousand manifestations
Arise and disappear
Without any reason.

Partly because his enlightenment experiences were connected to various Buddhist works (including the Surangama and Avatamsaka Sutras), and in any case following the tendency of the age, Han Shan did not strictly distinguish between Buddhist sects, fusing Ch'an with the inclusive view of Hua Yen, esoteric Buddhism, and Confucianism. He is related to the Lin Chi sect, but was unable to find a master qualified to certify his enlightenment. Han Shan had disciples but had no desire for his transmission to be carried down in any official line or sect.

On Clear Mind describes the method of practice from the state of self to the state of no-self. This is very good for the beginning practitioner but does not represent the highest level of Ch'an. Han Shan wrote the poem for a beginning student asking for guidance. Han Shan likens the mind to muddy water — in order to calm our mind we have to keep it perfectly still so that the mud will settle to the bottom, leaving the

Han Shan likens the mind to muddy water — in order
to calm our mind we have to keep it perfectly still so
that the mud will settle to the bottom, leaving the
water clear. The important thing is not to allow waves
of vexation to stir up the mud again. If there is a self,
the turbulence in the outer realm will cause your
mind to move. The mind emptied of self will naturally
be calm and peaceful, impervious to any obstruction.
You will feel free and independent, and as far as you
are concerned, nothing can transcend it.

Contemplating Mind also deals with the approach
one should take towards the practice; but it goes
further and describes the situation of the mind after
enlightenment. Most of the poem discusses the
method of contemplating the emptiness, yet complete-
ness, of the mind. Han Shan advises the practitioner to
avoid all attachments that may arise from meditation,
whether they be emotions, thoughts, or pleasant and
fearsome states. Instead one should concentrate on the
method of awareness because, "If you can see a
thought as it arises, this awareness will at once destroy it." But then Han Shan says that this method
itself must be discarded as soon as the mind is puri-
fied, or enlightened. At this point one will realize the
great powers and perfection inherent in the mind,
which is nothing other than the Buddha.

On Clear Mind

True nature is pure and deep
Like clear still water.
If beaten with hate or love
Waves of vexation arise.
Arising without cease
Self-nature becomes turbid.
Vexations and ignorance
Ever increase unconsciously.

Self grasping another
Is like mud entering water.
Self moved by another
Is like throwing fat on the fire.
While the outer realm is chaos, self is true.
When chaos is taken to be real, self is born.
If self is not born
Vexations, burning for eons, turn to ice.

Thus perfected ones
First empty the defilement of self.
When the defilement of self is emptied
How can the outer realm be an obstruction?
Resilience is the function
Of the self forgotten.
As soon as idiosyncracies appear
You recognize them immediately.

The point of recognition is enlightenment.
The instant one thought returns to brightness
All traces are swept away.
That moment is refreshing.
Refreshing, quiescent,
Peerless, independent,
Tranquil, harmonious.
Nothing can match it.

Contemplating Mind

Look upon the body as unreal,
An image in a mirror, the reflection of the moon in
    water.
Contemplate the mind as formless,
Yet bright and pure.

Not a single thought arising,
Empty, yet perceptive; still, yet illuminating;
Complete like the Great Emptiness,
Containing all that is wonderful.

Neither going out nor coming in,
Without appearance or characteristics,
Countless skillful means
Arise out of one mind.

Independent of material existence,
Which is ever an obstruction,
Do not cling to deluded thoughts.
These give birth to illusion.

Attentively contemplate this mind,
Empty, devoid of all objects.
If emotions should suddenly arise,
You will fall into confusion.

In a critical moment bring back the light,
Powerfully illuminating.
Clouds disperse, the sky is clear,
The sun shines brilliantly.

If nothing arises within the mind,
Nothing will manifest without.
That which has characteristics
Is not original reality.

If you can see a thought as it arises,
This awareness will at once destroy it.
Whatever state of mind should come,
Sweep it away, put it down.

Both good and evil states
Can be transformed by mind.
Sacred and profane appear
In accordance with thoughts.

Reciting mantras or contemplating mind
Are merely herbs for polishing a mirror.
When the dust is removed,
They are also wiped away.

Great extensive spiritual powers
Are all complete within the mind.
The Pure Land or the Heavens
Can be travelled to at will.

CONTEMPLATING MIND

You need not seek the real,
Mind originally is Buddha.
The familiar becomes remote,
The strange seems familiar.

Day and night,
Everything is wonderful.
Nothing you encounter confuses you.
These are the essentials of mind.

Books by Chan Master Sheng Yen from Shambhala

Attaining the Way: A Guide to the Practice of Chan Buddhism

A landmark guide to Chan practice that includes texts from Master Sheng Yen as well as three of his dharma ancestors going back to medieval times: Yuanyun Jiexian, Yuanlai, and Xuyun.

Complete Enlightenment: Zen Comments on the Sutra of Complete Enlightenment

Complete enlightenment is right here, right now, wherever you are, according to this central text of Chinese Buddhism. This is the first authoritative translation with commentary of the sutra.

Dharma Drum: The Life and Heart of Chan Practice

A guide to Chan, accompanied by 180 of Master Sheng Yen's gemlike sayings and aphorisms that serve as wonderful inspirations to practice.

The Infinite Mirror: Commentaries on Two Chan Classics

A pair of teaching poems from the Soto Zen tradition, demystified and made accessible for modern students.

Faith in Mind: A Commentary on Seng Ts'an's Classic

One of the briefest Zen texts—and one of the most beloved—revealed as a supremely practical source of guidance for spiritual practice.

The Poetry of Enlightenment: Poems by Ancient Chan Masters

Poetry as teaching: These verses by great masters of Chan, presented here by Master Sheng Yen, put us in direct contact with their enlightened mind.

Song of Mind: Wisdom from the Zen Classic Xin Ming

An accessible approach to yet another of the Zen classics— in the form of a week-long retreat led by Master Sheng Yen.